Table of Contents

Page

DISCLAIMER

Executive Summary

Title: Israel: Strategic Asset or Strategic Liability?

Author: Major Keith Tighe, United States Marine Corps

Thesis: A realistic understanding of the history of the Modern Middle East and U.S. strategic interests in that region combined with a thorough questioning of the historical U.S.-Israel alliance reveals that to a large extent, Israel is a strategic liability to the U.S.

Discussion: Since the U.S first recognized the state of Israel in 1948 U.S.-Israel relations have been close. The U.S. has supported Israel with billions of dollars in the form of grants and loans, the latest American technology and weaponry, as well as steadfast political backing against Israel's Arab neighbors. Proponents of the U.S.-Israel alliance argue that Israel is a strategic asset to the U.S. and that the strategic partnership that exists between the two states is necessary for the success of U.S. foreign policy in the region. The historical record with regard to the establishment of the original Palestine Mandate shows that Western imperialism played a significant role in stripping the Palestinian people of the ancestral homeland for expedient and political reasons. Further, U.S. support for the creation of the state of Israel in the United Nations, largely due to domestic political concerns, only shifted the base of Western interference in Arab lands from Britain to the U.S. and it is this interference that has created so much anti-Americanism throughout the Middle East. This study seeks to explore all facets of the U.S-Israel alliance in order to determine the strategic value of Israel to the U.S.

Conclusion: After giving Israel billions of dollars since 1948, provoking Soviet influence in the Middle East which almost brought the U.S. to the brink of nuclear war in 1973, suffering multiple attacks by al Qaeda, and fighting a costly war in Afghanistan to counter radical Islam, the reality lies closer to the characterization of Israel as a strategic liability.

Acknowledgments

I extend my deepest thanks to Dr. Edward Erickson for his encouragement, patience, and guidance as he helped me complete this project. Were it not for his mentorship throughout the process, it is unlikely I would have finished this work. I would also like to thank Lieutenant Colonel Frode Ommunson for his leadership and guidance. His professionalism and advice provided me with a true example of military excellence. I will be forever grateful to both of these fine gentlemen.

Israel is one of America's closest allies and has been since its creation in 1948. In fact, the U.S. is largely responsible for passage of the U.N resolution that created the state of Israel and it was the U.S. that first recognized Israel on May 15, 1948. Since then, Israel has been a steadfast ally of the U.S. and American and Israeli politicians alike tout the relationship between the two states as one of democratic like-mindedness and strategic importance. Historically, the concept of Israel as a strategic asset to the U.S. was based on the premise that an alliance with Israel was crucial in countering Soviet influence in the Middle East. Post Cold War, proponents of the U.S.-Israel alliance have argued that Israel is a strategic asset to the U.S. as both nations fight the rising tides of radical Islam and terrorism directed against them. Both of these views are at best outdated and at worst completely false and have the causal relationships backwards.

On close review of the historical record prior to the collapse of the Soviet Union in 1991, a solid argument can be made that rather than serving to counter expanding Soviet influence in the Middle East, the U.S. alliance with Israel served to invite Soviet influence in the region. Further, after the collapse of the Soviet Union, the U.S. did not come to the conclusion that it suddenly needed Israel as a strategic asset against terrorism or radical Islam. The alliance and "strategic" relationship already existed. It was, in fact, this pre-existing U.S.-Israel partnership that led al Qaeda to target the U.S in several attacks. Those who favor the axiom that Israel is a strategic asset to the U.S. have shifted the structural argument of Israel's "strategic asset" status from one reason to another without understanding the nature of the alliance and the impact it has in the Middle East. Again, proponents of the idea that Israel is a strategic asset to the U.S have the causal relationship reversed. Israel is not a strategic asset because the U.S. needed the Israelis to counter the Soviets or terrorism. Rather, the U.S provoked both Soviet influence in the Middle East as well as anti-Americanism and terror attacks such as 9/11 because of the alliance with Israel. A realistic understanding of the history of the Modern Middle East and U.S. strategic interests in that region combined with a thorough questioning of the historical U.S.-Israel alliance reveals that to a large extent, Israel is a strategic liability to the U.S.

Origins of Palestine

For centuries, the Ottoman Empire ruled over the great majority of the Mediterranean and the surrounding land including what would become the Palestine Mandate. During World War I, Britain, France, and Russia made an agreement in order to secure their respective strategic interests in the area, namely oil for Britain and France and access to the Mediterranean Sea for Russia. The Sykes-Picot Agreement, as it came to be known, divided up the conquered Ottoman Empire among the allied victors with Syria and Lebanon going to the French and Mesopotamia and Palestine going to the British. Mesopotamia, comprised of three Ottoman provinces, the Sunni Kurds in Mosul to the North; the Sunni Arabs in Baghdad in the middle; and the Shia Arabs in Basra to the South was conglomerated, renamed Iraq and granted final independence in 1932 after Britain realized the futility of trying to control the Mandate.[1] The Palestine Mandate was originally comprised of the current countries of Israel and Jordan but the British divided the Mandate into two parts along the Jordan River. The eastern part became Transjordan and was granted independence from British rule in 1922 while Britain maintained control over the Western part, known as Palestine, until 1948.[2] As the British began to allow Jews to immigrate to Palestine in fulfillment of the prophecy of a return to the Holy

Land, attempts to set up a government acceptable to both Jews and Arabs failed. The Palestinian Arabs saw the Jews as invaders, while the Jews considered Palestine their home as promised by God.

Zionism

Zionism has its foundation in the Jewish belief that the fulfillment of God's promise to the Jews lay in the establishment of the Kingdom of Israel in the Holy Land, or Palestine. Jews, who originally lived in and around Jerusalem and Palestine in general, fled their lands when conquering Roman Legions invaded the region. Thereafter spread throughout much of Europe, Jews believed that God sanctioned a return to Palestine and they envisioned this return to their ancestral lands along with the creation of a sovereign Jewish state as sanctioned by God. As centuries passed, more pressing concerns also emerged which would play a key role in the creation of the modern Zionist movement. Jews across Europe were barred from certain professions, universities, government jobs, and were restricted from living in many non-Jewish areas.[3] Coupled with the perceived promise from God, religious persecution in their adoptive states gave birth in the late 19th century to an emerging Zionist movement that would rapidly and effectively focus its influence in Europe and the Unites States in order to achieve its goal of a sovereign Jewish state in Palestine.

Modern political Zionism, which is best described as "Jewish nationalism focusing on Palestine"[4] has its roots in pre-Soviet Russia. There, anti-Semitic sentiment was strong and Jewish groups began forming with the intent of supporting Jewish settlement in Palestine.[5] According to Cleveland, Vladimir Jabotinski, Russian Jew and the founder of revisionist Zionism, "called for massive Jewish immigration into Palestine and the immediate proclamation of a Jewish commonwealth."[6] Additionally, Cleveland notes that "[Jabotinski] claimed that historic Palestine included Trans-Jordan and insisted that large-scale Jewish colonization take place in that territory."[7] A telling platform in Jabotinski's Revisionist Zionism stated that "Palestine is a territory whose chief geographical feature is this: that the river Jordan does not delineate its frontier, but flows through its center."[8] The scope and fervor of Zionism in its quest for a Jewish state is readily apparent in these passages and points to the construction of the Arab-Israeli conflict and the resultant destabilization of the Middle East as being the result of uncompromising policies of Zionism with the backing of western powers.

Globally, Zionism was slow to gain traction prior to World War I. Palestine, part of the Ottoman Empire at the time, fell under the rule of Sultan Abdul Hamid II. The Sultan did not support the immigration of large populations of European Jews into Ottoman lands and this, coupled with European and American hesitancy to support Zionism, contained the aspirations of the more ardent progenitors of Zionism.[9] Once the Ottoman Empire entered World War I on the side of Germany, the Western Allies began to plan the partitioning of Ottoman territory and this led to a softening of British sentiment towards Zionism. The British began to court the American and Russian Jewry under the hopes that Jewish contingents in these countries would influence both nations to support the war against Germany. With the determined help of Dr. Chaim Weizmann, the Zionist spokesman in Britain, Zionists took advantage of Britain's desire to influence America and Russia and they were successful in achieving a British proclamation supporting Zionist goals in Palestine.[10]

There were several reasons for the British backing of a Jewish state in Palestine. Chief among them was the British government's belief that American and Russian Jews should be courted in attempts to influence the governments of the U.S. and Russia to support Britain against Germany during World War I, which was raging across Europe at the time.[11] If the British could show that they supported Zionism, then Jews in America and Russia might be persuaded to pressure their respective governments to support Britain in the war. Arabs opposed the creation of a Jewish state on several grounds. First, the Arab states were growing weary of Western power and influence in their region and they interpreted, correctly, the creation of a Jewish state as another attempt by Britain to control Arabs and exert influence in the Middle East.[12] Also, Arabs in Palestine were promised an independent Arab state in exchange for a revolt against the Ottoman Empire during World War I in the Husayn-McMahon Correspondence.[13] This promise was made to Sharif Husayn of Mecca, the official guardian of Mecca and Medina, through a series of letters with Ronald Storrs and Henry McMahon, two British officials in Cairo.[14] The general tone of the agreement contained in the Husayn-McMahon Correspondence was that if Husayn led a revolt against the Ottoman Empire, Britain would grant Arab independence in lands specified in the letters.[15] Further tension was created by David Ben-Gurion, a hardline proponent of the creation of a Jewish sovereign state in Palestine, and his comments highlighted the negative effects of such arbitrary state creationism. As Smith relates: "[Ben-Gurion] made a nearly absolute distinction between Israel and the world Jewry on the one hand, and the goyim, or non-Jews, on the other. If the latter did not fulfill their perceived obligations to Israel, they would be at best ignored, at worst be fought."[16] Through the arbitrary creation of the state of Israel, the Western powers had planted the seeds for conflict in that the Arabs could neither be expected to submit to Israeli domination nor, further, to fulfill obligations the Israelis perceived were owed them by the non-Jews of the world as suggested by Ben-Gurion.

The Balfour Declaration of 1917 finally gave political life to Zionism and was instrumental in strengthening the connection between American Jews and Zionists as well as increasing Western support for the Zionist objective of a sovereign Jewish state in Palestine. While the Balfour Declaration was criticized by all parties involved as confusing and ambiguous, it opened the door to Jewish immigration into Palestine once Jerusalem fell to the British in December 1917. Palestine was ruled by the British military until 1920 when, at the San Remo Conference, Britain was given the mandate to rule the area and a civilian administration replaced existing military control. For the next twenty-eight years under the British mandate, the Jewish population in Palestine increased from around 93,000 to almost 600,000.[17] Tensions between the native Arabs in Palestine and immigrating Jews grew, sparking two episodes of violence and culminated in the White Paper of 1939, another British attempt to make some sense of the untenable situation in Palestine. The White Paper placed severe limitations on Jewish immigration into Palestine and stated that the British government no longer supported the creation of a Jewish sovereign state and that Palestine would be granted independence by 1949.[18] Neither the Jews nor Arabs were happy with the White Paper but as World War II began, the Palestinian Mandate and the future of Zionism were relegated to secondary status.

UN Resolution 181 - Origins of Israel

Several events during World War II played a crucial role in the future of Palestine. Hitler's extermination of millions of Jews was arguably the most significant and was instrumental in bringing sympathy to the plight of the European Jews and sparked a general undercurrent of support for establishing a Jewish homeland in Palestine.[19] The American Emergency Committee for Zionist Affairs convened a conference in 1942 at the Biltmore Hotel in New York in order to address unfolding events in Europe and promulgate a new Zionist program.[20] The conference signaled an important shift in the "world Jewish focus from Europe to the Unites States."[21] But the shift was more than geographic; the Biltmore Program, as the proposals adopted by the conference came to be known, also portended a shift from moderate Zionism led by Dr. Chaim Weizmann, the European leader of the Zionist movement, to a hardline call for a sovereign Jewish state in Palestine led by David Ben-Gurion, the leader of the Palestinian Zionists.[22] The proposals adopted by the conference came to be known as the Biltmore Program and called for, among other demands, the withdrawal of the British White Paper, unlimited Jewish immigration into Palestine, creation of a Jewish army, and the creation of a "Jewish Commonwealth" in Palestine.[23]

As the extent of Nazi war crimes against the Jews became more apparent throughout the course of the war, Jewish sentiment against the British, who still clung to the mandates of the White Paper, increased and the American Jewish Lobby began a campaign in earnest to sway U.S. politicians to the side of Zionism. Up to 1943, U.S. policy regarding the Palestine question was simply that "…[it] was a British responsibility."[24] Late in 1943, the American Jewish Conference, comprised of delegates from nearly every American national Jewish organization, presented U.S. Secretary of State Cordell Hull with a set of its resolutions supporting the Biltmore Program.[25] The Jewish Lobby had begun to turn political and popular sentiment in America toward support for the creation of a Jewish state in Palestine along three lines of effort: First, the humanitarian plight of the European Jews; second, the fulfillment of biblical prophecy; and third, as a democratic state in the Middle East.[26] The U.S. government was soon receiving dramatic amounts of telegrams and correspondence from the American Jewish lobby.[27]

Under the weight of intensive Jewish lobbying and in response to a letter from King Saud of Saudi Arabia, President Roosevelt responded, "It is the view of the Government of the United States that no decision altering the basic situation of Palestine should be reached without full consultation with both Arabs and Jews."[28] United States foreign policy up to the end of World War II had generally been one of non-interference in the affairs of other nation-states. The U.S. Director of the Office of Near-Eastern and African Affairs, Loy Henderson, succinctly stated this policy in an August 1945 memo to Secretary of State James Byrnes:

> …in our considered opinion the active support by the Government of the United States of a policy favoring the setting up of a Jewish State in Palestine would be contrary to the policy which the United States has always followed of respecting the wishes of a large majority of the local inhabitants with respect to their form of government. Furthermore it would have a strongly adverse effect upon American interests throughout the Near and Middle East…[29]

Thus was set the first official U.S. foreign policy regarding Palestine and it would remain so until President Harry Truman drastically changed it in 1946.

In April 1946, a joint American-British committee released a set of recommendations regarding the Palestine question. The report called for, among other concessions, the immediate immigration of 100,000 Jews into Palestine. In perhaps one of the most drastic foreign policy shifts in American history, President Truman publically supported the findings of the committee. The impact of Truman's public call for large-scale Jewish immigration into Palestine was not lost on the Arab states surrounding Palestine. The Near-East division of the U.S. State Department reported that Syria, Lebanon, Egypt, and Saudi Arabia were all registering criticism, disillusionment, and intentions to resist Truman's new position on Palestine.[30] Britain was also very displeased since Truman's call for what amounted to open immigration of Jews into Palestine was in direct contradiction to their own policy regarding the Palestinian mandate they were responsible for. Various Jewish elements within Palestine, having been relatively quiet and peaceful during the immediate post-war period seized the opportunity presented by the lack of unity between the U.S. and Britain. Zionist militant groups including the Irgun, Lehi, and Haganah increased their attacks against British security forces and Arabs settlements in a bid to force British acceptance of a Jewish state. On February 14 1947, Britain, plagued by violence in Palestine and criticism from both Jews and Arabs and at odds with President Harry Truman over immigration of more Jews into Palestine, handed the future of Palestine to the United Nations.[31] The United Nations General Assembly created the Special Committee on Palestine (UNSCOP) to formulate recommendations on the disposition of Palestine. UNSCOP determined that the British mandate should end and that Palestine be granted independence, however, the commission was divided on the form of government the new state should have. A majority report, backed by the U.S.,[32] called for the partitioning of Palestine into Jewish and Arab states and a minority report recommended a federal state. The entire issue of the

UNSCOP report came to a vote on 29 November 1947, wherein the General Assembly passed the majority opinion as Resolution 181. Officially, Resolution 181 called for the partitioning of Palestine between an Arab state, a Jewish state, and the city of Jerusalem.[33] The resolution also allowed for the immigration of 150,000 Jews over a two-year period and granted the Negev, Eastern Galilee, and most of the coastline to The Jews. Arab Palestinians were awarded the mountain region of the Palestinian heartland, Gaza Strip, and Western Galilee. Arab reaction to Resolution 181 was swift. American diplomatic missions in Baghdad and Damascus were attacked; King Farouk of Egypt stated to the U.S. Ambassador in Cairo that the Arab states would use force to prevent the partition; and Walid Khalidi, a Palestinian scholar, voiced Palestinian Arab opinion:

> The Palestinians failed to see why they should be made to pay for the Holocaust. They failed to see why it was *not* fair for the Jews to be a minority in a unitary Palestinian state, while it *was* fair for almost half of the Palestinian population - the indigenous majority on its own ancestral soil – to be converted overnight into a minority under alien rule in the envisaged Jewish state according to partition.[34]

Britain, who abstained from voting, was also displeased with Resolution 181 and announced the withdrawal of its 100,000 troops by 15 May 1948 thus completely washing their hands of the matter. The Jews quickly moved to fill the void left as the British pulled out and fighting quickly broke out between Zionists and Arabs. It quickly became apparent that armed intervention was the only way to keep the two sides apart and the U.S., as the biggest sponsor of Resolution 181 and partition, would be required to provide the military support to keep the peace. The possibility of the U.S. military fighting the Palestinian Arabs in order to take their land and give it to the Jews as directed by the U.N. and Resolution 181 was exactly what the U.S. State Department had feared. The Policy Planning Staff stated: "[U.S. military intervention] would in Arab eyes be a virtual declaration of war by the U.S. against the Arab world."[35]

Within months of the U.N. plan to partition Palestine, the British had withdrawn, Jews had begun to forcibly take land promised to them by Resolution 181, thousands of Palestinian Arabs were fled their homes or were forced out by the advancing Jews, and Arab states in the region were threatening war. Arabs in the states surrounding Palestine "emphatically rejected"[36] the partition and Palestinian Arabs refused to accept or implement Resolution 181 on the grounds they considered it illegal and tantamount to the Western powers stealing their land and giving it to the Jews. [37] The United States was paralyzed and reluctant to send military forces in to enforce the partition that it had engineered and the Jews, armed and well trained, prepared to expand the borders assigned to them in the Resolution.[38] On 14 May 1948 as the situation deteriorated rapidly, Israel declared its independence and the United States immediately recognized the new state of Israel. The surrounding Arab states, angry over Western imperialism and interference, attacked.

Arab-Israeli Wars 1948, 1956, 1967, 1973

On May 15, 1948, armies from Syria, Lebanon, Jordan, Egypt, and Iraq invaded the new Jewish state of Israel. Poorly trained, equipped, and led, the Arab coalition also lacked any appreciable coordination and were out-numbered by their Jewish opponent.[39] Numbering approximately 30,000 troops against the Arabs 21,000,[40] the Israelis successfully defended against the attack and expanded their territory beyond the borders outlined in Resolution 181.[41] The Israelis, executing what they called Plan Dalet or "Plan D", terrorized the remaining Arab population within Israeli borders into leaving their land and homes, forcefully expelled those Arabs who would not leave, and leveled the Arab towns and villages.[42] When the armistice was concluded with each attacking Arab state in 1949, any semblance of a Palestinian state vanished and over 700,000 Palestinians became refugees.[43] Israel controlled seventy-seven percent of Palestine, Egypt held the Gaza Strip, and Jordan possessed the territory west of the Jordan River known as the West Bank.[44] Thus, the beginning of the contemporary Arab-Israeli conflict can be traced to the cessation of hostilities between the newly formed state of Israel and the Arab states of Iraq, Lebanon, Egypt, Jordan, and Syria.[45] The conclusion of the war in 1948 and the adoption of the armistice agreements between Israel and the Arab states in 1949 ushered in an era of uneasy truce in which neither peace nor war existed.[46]

Between 1949 and 1956, tension remained high between the Arab world and Israel. According to Smith, the informal Israeli policy of retaliation against Arab countries that refused to control Palestinian Arab attempts to return to their homes in Israel led to "increased hostilities with the Arab governments rather than encouraging a receptivity to negotiations."[47] In what can only be described as events resembling a story line from one of Ian Fleming's "007" novels, Israel invaded Egypt in 1956.

The Israelis, constantly afraid of another Egyptian attack from the Sinai Peninsula, attempted to bomb the American and British embassies in Cairo using Egyptian Jews. Israel's intent was to undermine Egyptian security and prompt the British to re-think removing their army from the Sinai. Egyptian authorities caught the would-be bombers prior to the attack and hung them but Israeli involvement was not discovered. In a characteristic act of reprisal, Israel raided an Egyptian army base in Gaza, killing over fifty Egyptian soldiers. Nasser responded to Israel's raid by requesting an arms deal with the U.S., which President Eisenhower refused out of fear that U.S weapons would be used against Israel. Nasser next turned to the Soviet Union for help and purchased arms from the Soviets via Czechoslovakia, which in turn sparked a series of events that culminated with an Israeli invasion of Egypt in October 1956 supported by Britain and France.[48] In retaliation for the Soviet-Egyptian arms deal, the U.S. withdrew an offer to finance the Aswan Dam project in Egypt, complicating an already delicate relationship; Egypt and the U.S. were already at odds as a result of Nasser's recognition of communist China in May 1956, when funding of the Aswan Dam project was canceled.[49] Nasser, in a political bid to confront the U.S. and display Egyptian sovereignty, nationalized the Suez Canal on July 26, 1956. Britain and France both wanted Nasser removed from power and they used the nationalization of the canal as the justification for invading.[50] Instigated by the French but assisted by the British, both countries conspired with Israel to regain control of the canal in October 1956. Israel would attack through the Sinai Peninsula toward the Suez Canal. Britain and France would "protect" the canal by landing peacekeeping forces to keep the Egyptian and Israeli armies away from it, thus rendering the waterway open to world commerce and out of Egyptian control.[51]

Israel attacked on schedule while British and French forces waited off the coast of Egypt.[52] As Israeli forces pressed their attack toward the canal, Britain and France called for a truce and demanded that both Israel and Egypt withdrawal to ten miles away from the Suez Canal. The idea was to allow Israel to continue their attack up to that line while forcing Egypt to withdrawal all their forces from the Sinai Peninsula. Since the Sinai was

Egyptian territory, Britain and France assumed Nasser would not agree to the demand, which would then allow British and French forces to land and wrest control of the canal from the Egyptians. The plan worked well and while Israel failed to acquire any new territory in the attack they destroyed a large quantity of Egyptian equipment.[53] Of greater significance, Israel destroyed the Egyptian artillery at Sharm al-Shaykh, which opened the Strait of Tiran to Israeli shipping through the Red Sea into the Gulf of Aqaba.[54] Israel then managed to secure a promise from the U.S. to keep the Strait of Tiran open and the placement of a U.N. Emergency Force (UNEF) on the Egyptian side of the border in order to prevent further conflict.[55] Further, Israel threatened that any future attempt by Egypt to re-occupy the positions at Sharm al-Shaykh and blockade the Tiran Strait would be "casus belli."[56] Although the U.S. opposed the Franco-British action in the war and demanded they withdraw from Egypt, contemporary Western support of Israel and perceived interference in Arab lands now officially extended beyond the issue of Palestine and the United States was drawn into the dispute in support of Israel.

For the next eleven years tensions continued to flare between Israel and her Arab neighbors. Border clashes between Israel and Syria, in particular, precipitated the war in 1967, also known as the Six Day War.[57] Israeli incursions into Arab controlled territory prompted Syrian shelling into Israel and as tensions escalated, Syria called on Nasser of Egypt to intercede.[58] In May of 1967, in response to Syrian demands for help, Nasser began mobilizing his forces, ordered the UNEF out of the Sinai, and closed the Tiran Straits to Israeli ships. On May 30 Jordan signed a three-way pact with Syria and Egypt, sparking another Israeli attack that came on June 5. Within six days, Israel had defeated the Egyptian Air Force, destroyed Egyptian armor in the Sinai, moved back to the Suez

Canal, taken control of the entire West Bank from Jordan including Jerusalem, and seized the Golan Heights from Syria.[59] In a tacit gesture of approval and support, the U.S. urged Israel to conclude their attacks quickly in order to prevent the Soviets from sending troops into the fight, as they promised to do.[60] Acting surreptitiously, the Johnson administration in Washington gave unofficial support to Israel's plan of attack between 25 to 30 May, however, after 30 May, this support became public and official when the U.S. Ambassador to the United Nations delivered a message of support to Israel on President Johnson's behalf.[61] While Israel had full knowledge of U.S. support for its plan to attack, Egypt and the rest of the Arab states knew nothing. In fact, Smith points out that "[The] Egyptians would later make the point that Washington advised them to hold back [their own attack] until a diplomatic resolution was reached while encouraging Israel to attack."[62] The Americans had once again sided with Israel against the Arab world. Further, they convinced the Arabs to delay any attack against Israel while secretly encouraging Israel to go to war. Israel now occupied the Gaza Strip, Golan Heights, and the West Bank, which precipitated a massive exodus of Palestinians into surrounding Arab states. In effect, what remained of Palestinian territory prior to 1967 was now occupied by Israel and the Palestinians themselves were either forced to live under Israeli occupation or become refugees elsewhere.

By October 1973, tensions between Israel and the surrounding Arab States once again led to war. In the years between 1967 and 1973, clashes occurred regularly between the two sides generally centered on Israeli occupied territory seized in the 1967 war. From its position of strength post 1967, Israel was not convinced to enter into talks with Syria or Egypt regarding the land taken in that war. Anwar Sadat wished to improve

Egypt's bargaining position in the case of talks but was frustrated by Soviet indifference to a settlement plan. In a bid to garner U.S. support for a settlement initiative with Israel, Sadat ordered Soviet troops and advisors out of Egypt in July 1972.[63] Unfortunately for the prospects of peace, U.S. Secretary of State Henry Kissinger, who had previously indicated that the U.S. would only support peace talks if Egypt expelled the Soviets, failed to respond to Sadat's overture. With the prospect of peace talks seemingly at an impasse, Egypt and Syria ordered their forces to attack. Egyptian forces overran the Israeli Bar-Lev line along the Suez Canal while Syrian forces almost broke through Israel's defenses in the Golan Heights. Israeli forces regrouped and counter-attacked on both fronts, quickly retaking lost ground and seizing even more territory than it had prior to the start of hostilities.[64] The U.S. attempted to negotiate a cease-fire but Egypt refused. In response to Egypt's refusal, the U.S. provided large weapons shipments and $2.2 billion in emergency financial aid to Israel. Saudi Arabia's King Faysal, who had warned Washington of the impending war in an attempt to force the U.S. to pressure Israel into peace talks, called for the Organization of Petroleum Exporting Countries (OPEC) to begin an oil embargo and reduce production in retaliation for this American support to Israel.[65] Israel, Syria, and Egypt agreed to a cease-fire on October 22 and negotiations for a full settlement began shortly thereafter.

Review of U.S. Activity

Shortly after the Suez invasion of 1956 it became clear to Washington that, as the British and French declined in the Middle East, a power vacuum would leave the area vulnerable to Soviet influence. With a large percentage of the world's oil supply in the region, President Eisenhower was reluctant to cede any amount of power or influence in

Arab states to the Soviets. Though Egypt's Nasser had approached the U.S. for aid prior to the Suez crisis, Washington denied the help, forcing Nasser to court Soviet assistance. U.S. politicians and the American public, in turn, viewed this as a sign of Soviet influence in the region supported by Egypt which was exactly what Eisenhower sought to avoid.[66] Consequently and perhaps in an ironic turn of fate, Eisenhower formulated a doctrine to counter the very Soviet influence his administration had forced Egypt into accepting. The Eisenhower Doctrine, as it came to be known, sought to bolster the more moderate Arab states and counter Nasser as well as any further Soviet influence in the region. The doctrine, approved by Congress in March 1957, promised economic and military aid to any nation who requested assistance and even included provisions for the use of American military forces.[67] After chastising Britain and France for attempting to overthrow Nasser, the U.S. was actively encouraging other Arab states to request American military help for the same purpose.[68] In effect, the lines had been drawn in the Middle East and, with Britain and France sidelined with respect to security concerns, Eisenhower was determined to assume the mantle of power in order to prevent Soviet expansion and influence in the region.[69] As Smith summarizes, "The United States now embarked on a period of active intervention in Arab regional politics that in the long run led it closer to Israel."[70] Eisenhower believed the best way to manage the Middle East was through maintaining the status quo and that meant that Egypt and Jordan controlled the Gaza Strip and West Bank respectively while Israel's borders should remain intact from the peace agreement of 1949.[71]

The Eisenhower doctrine continued in practice if not in name throughout the Kennedy and Johnson administrations. However, several key events occurred during the

1960s, which exacerbated the problems in the Middle East and helped bring U.S. political and popular support more in line with Israel's position. Adolph Eichmann, the Nazi architect of the "final solution", was tried for war crimes in Israel in 1961 and his trial served to galvanize support for Israel in the U.S. both politically as well as with the public.[72] As Christison points out, Eichmann's trial exposed the brutality of the Holocaust and generated newfound sympathy in America for the survival of Israel but another less obvious effect was the vilification of the Palestinians as the prosecutor drew links between the Mufti of Jerusalem and the Nazis.[73] Additionally, the Six-Day War in 1967 played a very important role in shaping future U.S. policy on the issue of Israel and Palestine.

President Johnson, influenced heavily by the Israelis, adopted the stance that Israel would not be forced to return the territory it seized during the Six-Day War unless the surrounding Arab states agreed to "…full and permanent peace."[74] While not suggesting that Israel had the right to occupy permanently the areas taken during the war, the policy did not address Palestinian sovereignty or refugees but called for a guarantee of peace from the Arabs.[75] In effect, the U.S. was assisting Israel with its goals while ignoring the basic complaints of the Palestinian people and demanding concessions from Syria, Egypt, and Jordan. Out of this position, U.N. Security Council Resolution 242 was passed in 1967, which called for Israeli withdrawal from the occupied territories, an end to "belligerency", recognition of borders, and resolution of the refugee issue.[76]

With the rise during the 1960s of Palestinian militant groups pushing popular sentiment in the U.S. away from Arabs and toward the Israelis and a prevailing fear of increased Soviet influence in the region, U.S. foreign policy in the Middle East tended to favor the Israelis over the Arab states.[77] Arab heads of state complicated the dynamic

when they vowed there would be no peace, no negotiations, and no recognition of Israel

after the war in 1967 and this, coupled with the U.S. fear of rising Soviet influence in the

region, would cause President Nixon to espouse a policy of "evenhandedness" which

sought to avoid the appearance of favoring either the Israelis or Arabs.

As the Cold War became paramount in the priorities of strategic thinkers, Nixon

felt that a balanced approach to both sides in the Arab-Israeli conflict would serve to

draw Arab states away from Soviet influence. Henry Kissinger, Nixon's National

Security Advisor at the time, believed otherwise. He felt the best way to counter the

Soviets was through reinforcing U.S. alliances in the region while undermining those

states allied with the Soviet Union. In effect, this meant favoring Israel over Arab states

that were aligned with the U.S.S.R.[78] As the primacy of countering the Soviets

supplanted the appearance of "evenhandedness" in the Middle East, Nixon gradually

ascribed to Kissinger's view and U.S. policy was thus set.[79]

In practice, this policy was tantamount to enforcing the status quo rather than a

serious attempt to resolve the issue and as Christison notes, "Indeed, in his first few years

in office Kissinger advocated that the United States specifically avoid any serious effort

to resolve the conflict, in the belief that stalemate was in the U.S. interest because it

would frustrate the radical Arabs and the Soviets."[80] Against the back-drop of increasing

terror attacks from groups like the Palestine Liberation Organization (PLO), U.S.

domestic politics, and the Cold War, U.S. activity during the Nixon and Ford

administrations heavily favored Israel while relegating Arab states to the decision of a

"your either with us or against us" choice.

The U.S. policies of this era exacerbated an already bad situation in the Middle East by pitting states in the region against each other under the auspices of halting Soviet influence. That the U.S. was also seen to heavily support Israel did not help to bring Arab sentiment to America's cause. Without a good faith attempt on the part of either the Nixon or Ford administrations to broker an honest peace agreement, which recognized the seizure of Arab territory and the displacement of the Palestinian people as the starting point for negotiations, nothing changed except for Arab resentment of the U.S., which grew. Christison characterizes the effect like this: "In its pursuit of stability, the [Nixon] administration failed to recognize that just beneath the surface frustrations were mounting in Egypt and Syria and among the Palestinians—were mounting in fact in direct proportion to the warmth of the U.S.-Israeli relationship."[81]

When Jimmy Carter became president in 1977, he began moving U.S. diplomatic efforts in the Middle East in a slightly different direction than his predecessors. He publicly asserted that the Palestinians were an essential part of the equation of achieving a peace agreement in the region.[82] Carter also pushed the idea of a Palestinian "homeland" and went so far as to suggest inclusion of the PLO in the peace process.[83] While Carter's attempt to bring a lasting peace to the Middle East was a departure from previous administrations, it ultimately failed. Significantly, however, Carter's recognition of the Palestinian people as an integral component of the peace process was remarkable in that it was the first time a U.S. president made this connection in the hopes of solving the ongoing enmity between Israel and the surrounding Arab states. As Christison points out:

…Carter was quite different from his predecessors in his desire, from the beginning, to explore new ideas and venture into new diplomatic territory and in his perception that a secure and stable Middle East peace would require what he called a "broader perspective." That expanded perspective encompassed the Arab and the Palestinian viewpoint. As one of his principal foreign-policy aides, former Assistant Secretary of State Harold Saunders, has noted, Carter came to office, almost alone among presidents, knowing there were two sides to the Arab-Israeli conflict.[84]

It was from this viewpoint that President Carter began a series of visits to the various states of the Middle East in an attempt to spark multilateral talks that he hoped would end in a peace agreement.[85]

While Jordan and Syria refused to engage in the talks for various reasons, Anwar Sadat of Egypt and Yitzhak Rabin of Israel were somewhat receptive to Carter's suggestion but remained skeptical of the multilateral framework proposed.[86] Both leaders preferred a bilateral agreement for political reasons; Sadat would gain U.S. economic support, which would stabilize Egypt, and negotiate the return of the Sinai Peninsula seized by Israel in the Six-Day War thus giving Sadat a huge political boost at home;[87] Israeli Prime Minister Menachem Begin envisioned a "divide and conquer" strategy of engaging in talks with Egypt without having to deal with the entire Arab coalition.

While the ongoing negotiations between Egypt and Israel were not the multilateral talks he had hoped for, Carter recognized the utility of the bilateral effort and called for a summit between the two sides. Pushed by his desire for progress on the issue and the increasing possibility that the talks already occurring between Begin and Sadat would fail to achieve an agreement, Carter convened what came to be known as the Camp David talks in September 1978.[88]

By most accounts the Camp David talks were successful and resulted in two sets of agreements. The first agreement centered on the West Bank and Gaza Strip and gave recognition to the "legitimate rights of the Palestinian people" and a process to achieve autonomy in these two area within five years. Interpretation of who, exactly, the Palestinian people were became an issue later when Begin indicated that "people" only meant those Palestinians already living in the two areas and not displaced refugees.[89] Sadat and Carter, however, thought all Palestinians were included in the definition thus allowing PLO participation in future processes.[90] This was an important distinction, which would have ramifications under President Ronald Reagan. The second agreement was the framework for a peace treaty that was signed by both sides in March 1979. Specifically addressed were the removal of Israeli forces and settlements from the Sinai Peninsula, guarantees of Israeli freedom of movement through the Suez Canal and Straits of Tiran, as well as limits on Egyptian military build-up in the Sinai.[91] Although the Camp David Accords were a step in the direction of peace and achieved recognition of the Palestinians as a people central to the larger issue of Arab-Israeli peace, much of the language contained in the Accords was ambiguous and left the issue of Israel's occupation of Jerusalem unaddressed as well as Israel's policy of refusing to allow Palestinian refugees to return to their ancestral lands in the occupied territories. This particular omission, considered a non-negotiable plank in Israeli policy, would have serious consequences with regard to Arab views of the U.S. years later. Additionally, much of the ambiguous language favored Israel[92] and with the election of Ronald Reagan in 1980, Carter's contribution to U.S. foreign policy in the Middle East was soon reversed.

The Reagan administration's approach to policy in the region was similar to that of the Nixon administration and neglected the issues of Palestinian nationalism and Israeli occupation of territory taken during the Six-Day War as key to solving the turmoil in the Middle East. Another similarity to pre-Carter policy was the attempt to build anti-Soviet coalitions between Israel and the western-leaning Arab states, in effect pitting Arab against Arab.[93] Unlike Carter who had least considered PLO participation in the peace process, the Reagan administration refused to recognize or negotiate with the organization. U.S. foreign policy toward the various Arab states under Reagan can be characterized as contradictory and divisive; the Reagan administration sold military aircraft to Saudi Arabia for defense against Iran, who was embroiled in a war with Iraq; leveraged Israel to sell arms to Iran, who then used them against Iraq; and provided information to Iraq regarding Iran's military movements.[94] The money acquired from the sale of U.S. arms to Iran was diverted for the purpose of countering Soviet influence in Central America, so in this regard Israel could loosely be considered a asset against the backdrop of the larger U.S. policy of countering Soviet expansion. However, this weapons for cash debacle, known as the Iran-Contra Affair, was illegal according to international and U.S. law and was not instrumental in defeating communist expansion in the region; therefore, this conclusion is dubious at best.

More recently, the administration of George W. Bush established good relations with Israel and adopted a supportive policy. In 2003 the administration agreed to provide Israel with nine billion dollars in loan guarantees spread out over several years.

Additionally, although the Bush administration did not agree with Israel's continued settlement of the occupied territories, President Bush's position on the issue of Palestinian lands showed strong support for the Israeli agenda. While supporting an end to Israeli construction and settlement in the disputed areas, Bush believed that a successful resolution to the problem was predicated on accepting new "realities on the ground" meaning prior Israeli settlement. This had the effect of disenfranchising Arabs in general and the Palestinians in particular because Bush was simultaneously calling on the Palestinian Authority to clamp down on terror elements attacking Israel from the occupied territory. In effect, the very issue at the heart of Palestinian anger, Israel's occupation and settlement of Palestinian lands, became the proverbial line in the sand once Bush sided with Israel. America was telling the Palestinian people to stop being angry about losing their homeland to Israel and to accept the seizure and settlement as a new "reality."

Although the Obama administration tends to support the Israelis, this support is less warm than that given by previous administrations. In a speech made in 2011, President Obama stated:

> So while the core issues of the conflict must be negotiated, the basis of those negotiations is clear: a viable Palestine, a secure Israel. The United States believes that negotiations should result in two states, with permanent Palestinian borders with Israel, Jordan, and Egypt, and permanent Israeli borders with Palestine. We believe the borders of Israel and Palestine should be based on the 1967 lines with mutually agreed swaps, so that secure and recognized borders are established for both states. The Palestinian people must have the right to govern

themselves, and reach their full potential, in a sovereign and contiguous state.[95] The next year, in a more concrete show of support for Israel, Obama renewed the US-Israeli guaranteed loan program started under Bush for another three years.[96]

Review of Current U.S. Policy

Current U.S. National Security Strategy (NSS) continues to seek a resolution to the greater Arab-Israeli conflict while also recognizing the plight of the Palestinian people and a two-state solution to that particular problem. President Obama's 2010 strategy highlights the importance of Israel as an ally and references that country as a "close friend" and reaffirms the U.S.'s "unshakable commitment to its security."[97] Although the current NSS seeks an end to the issue of Palestinian sovereignty through "…a Jewish state of Israel, with true security, acceptance, and rights for all Israelis; and a viable, independent Palestine with contiguous territory that ends the occupation that began in 1967…"[98], there is clear language in the document that unquestionably favors Israel as a friend and pre-eminent ally: "We have an array of enduring interests, longstanding commitments and new opportunities for broadening and deepening relationships in the greater Middle East. This includes maintaining a strong partnership with Israel while supporting Israel's lasting integration into the region."[99] No such language exists in the NSS with regard to either the Palestinians or the various Arab states and this characterization of the U.S-Israeli relationship while omitting a similar U.S.-Arab bond indicates a stronger U.S. commitment to Israel and the Israeli agenda.

Similarly, the National Defense Strategic Guidance of the U.S. published in January 2012 contains language that broadly refers to "Gulf security" and specifically mentions the U.S. commitment to Israeli security: "U.S. policy will emphasize Gulf security, in collaboration with Gulf Cooperation Council countries when appropriate, to prevent Iran's development of a nuclear weapon capability and counter its destabilizing policies. The United States will do this by standing up for Israel's security and a comprehensive Middle East peace."[100] Although this strategy aims at broad security cooperation across the Middle East, U.S. support for Israeli security is succinctly stated while leaving unclear exactly what American support consists of with regard to Arab states and their security in the region. Both the NSS and the 2012 Strategic Guidance provide assurances that Middle East peace figures prominently into U.S. global strategy; however, only Israel is singled out by name for special security concessions from the U.S. in these two documents.[101] Additionally, Israel is named twenty-two times in the NSS while all other Middle Eastern states surrounding Israel are mentioned a combined seven times.[102] The passage above from the 2012 Strategic Guidance names Israel specifically to assure that country of U.S. support but no other Arab state is mentioned a single time in the document.[103] With this in mind, it is clear that U.S. support to Israel is a higher priority than that to any other Middle Eastern state.

More tangible indications of U.S. support to Israel are evidenced by financial contributions, both in economic and military aid. Historically, the U.S. provided more aid to Israel in both categories combined than any other country.[104] The exceptions to this are Iraq, which received more aid from 2003 to 2009, and Afghanistan, which received more from 2005 to present.[105] These two anomalies are attributable to the wars the U.S. fought in both countries; however, this does not diminish the significance or meaning of the steady flow of U.S. funds to Israel. U.S. foreign aid to Israel has been growing steadily since the Jewish state's inception in 1948.[106] When compared to foreign aid given to all other nations in the Middle East and North Africa combined, the percentage given to

Israel for economic and military aid is extraordinary. From 1946 to 2011, Israel received

approximately 40 percent of all U.S. aid in the region.[107] While the amount of U.S aid to

Israel fluctuated between thirty-five million and one hundred million dollars annually

from 1949 to the early 1970s, Shannon indicates that the first major increase in aid to

Israel occurred in 1974 when the total skyrocketed to almost 2.5 billion dollars for the

year.[108] That this increase was tied directly to the war in 1973 is significant. Contrast this

with the prior year aid total of 480 million.[109] Again in 1979, as Shannon points out,

another spike in U.S. aid to Israel occurred and reached the unprecedented total of 4.9

billion dollars whereas the total for 1978 only reached 1.8 billion.[110] When viewed

against the backdrop of the 1973 War and OPEC oil embargo, both in 1973, and the

Iranian Revolution in January of 1979, the spikes in U.S. aid to Israel in 1974 and 1979

suggest the implication of Israel as a strategic asset to the U.S.

In addition to political speeches, documents pledging assistance, and economic

and military aid, the U.S. also maintains a robust set of formal agreements with Israel.

According to the Jewish Virtual Library website, there are fifty treaties, agreements, and

Memorandums of Understanding (MOU) between Israel and the U.S. in the areas of

economics, security, and defense.[111] Significant among these formal agreements are

several related to Israel's security; specifically, a 1988 agreement that designated Israel

as "a major, non-NATO ally of the United States"[112]; several agreements pertaining to

the Arrow anti-ballistic missile system from 1989 to 2009; and several counter-terror

agreements.[113] The Arrow missile agreements in particular resulted from Israel's desire to

build a surface-to-surface missile defense capability in order to counter Arab states that had previously attacked or possibly would attack Israel.[114] The "major ally" agreement with Israel gave significant concessions to Israel such as preferential treatment for contracts and low prices for U.S. military hardware.[115] The implication contained in these agreements is that the U.S. will assist Israel in defending itself against an attack by the surrounding Arab states if not with ground forces then with technology and military hardware.

Current Destabilizing Issues

Israeli occupation of Palestinian land continues to generate conflict and instability in the Middle East. Beginning with Israel's occupation before the war in 1948 of large portions of the territory set aside for Palestinians as part of the 1947 U.N. partition plan, Israel's seizure and continued occupation of Palestinian land has proven a major obstacle to peace in the region.[116] As Smith points out, "[Zionist leadership in April 1948] agreed that the Hagana should try to establish control of the zone granted to Jews by 15 May [1948] and to expand the area to include those Jewish settlements outside the [U.N.] partition lines."[117] In other words, the Jewish leadership wanted to take land identified as Palestinian b the U.N. if any Jews lived there. In a six-week period from April to May 15, 1948 the Hagana and Irgun attacked across the proposed partition lines into Palestinian villages and towns. By May 14 when Israel declared its sovereignty, more than 300,000 Palestinians abandoned their homes or were forcibly ejected as the Hagana pressed their attacks.[118] As quickly as the Palestinians fled, the Jews advanced and claimed the land for Israel having declared it "abandoned" by the former occupants. Israel claimed then and continues to hold to the position that the Palestinians left their land at the behest of neighboring Arab states and thus they are not refugees and have no right to return to the land they abandoned and it is this logic which Israel invokes when explaining why Israeli settlements are legal.[119]

Israel's occupation and settlement of territory set aside by the U.N. Partition Plan continues to provide a source of tension and conflict for Arabs and Israel.[120] Occupation of the West Bank and Jerusalem, in particular, complicate the peace process, as both sides appear unwilling to compromise their respective positions. Palestinians have long claimed that they have a right to return to their lands taken by Israel in the 1948 and 1967 wars while Israel refuses to relinquish the territory and continues to build settlements.[121] Israel did, however, begin a phased return of control of the Gaza Strip, which it occupied since the 1967 war, to the Palestinian Authority (PA) as a result of the 1994 Oslo Accords. The Israelis withdrew military control in the West bank to areas of Jewish settlement only, allowing the PA to police and administer the Palestinian areas of the strip and in 2005 the Israelis signed a unilateral disengagement plan with the PA and began a complete withdrawal of military forces and settlements from the Gaza Strip. Israel completed the withdrawal in September 2005, formally ending thirty-eight years of occupation but the issues of occupation and settlement of the West Bank and Jerusalem remain as drivers of regional instability.[122]

Another destabilizing issue in the region is the specter of a nuclear capable Iran. President Obama's recent visit to Israel and the West Bank in mid-March, 2013 highlighted the importance of this issue in the region. During a speech given on March 20, 2013 after meeting with Israeli Prime Minister Benjamin Netanyahu, President Obama told reporters that Israel's security is "non-negotiable" and a "solemn obligation" of America.[123] Israeli President Shimon Peres also weighed in on the possibility of a nuclear Iran and U.S. intentions and commitments. In an interview with Fox News on March 21, 2013, Peres indicated he believes President Obama will use military force against Iran if diplomacy fails to resolve the current standoff over Iranian nuclear ambitions.[124] Given the existing tension between Israel and Iran, President Obama's comments signify a definitive U.S. position: a commitment of U.S. military action against Iran in defense of Israel. President Obama clearly indicated Israel's status as a protectorate of the U.S. in case of an Iranian attack.

Analysis

Israel's position as a strategic asset to the U.S. is something of an axiom within U.S. and Israeli political circles. Historical thinking holds that Israel was a strategic asset to America during the Cold War as a counter to Soviet expansion and influence in the Middle East. Contrary to this belief, President Truman's own State Department opposed recognition of Israel in 1948 and felt that support to Israel would damage U.S. standing with Arab states and "facilitate Soviet penetration of the region."[125] George Kennan, head of policy planning for the U.S. State Department summarized in a 1948 memorandum: "Supporting the extreme objectives of political Zionism [would be] to the detriment of overall U.S. security objectives [in the Middle East]."[126] Kennan's characterization of the situation proved correct when Egypt turned to the Soviet Union for military and financial support in 1955 after the U.S. sided with Israel and denied President Nasser's request for help.

After Israel's 1955 attack on an Egyptian military base in Gaza, President Nasser appealed to the U.S. for the purchase of weapons. President Eisenhower refused, concerned that these weapons might be used in an eventual attack on Israel and in an ironic twist of fate, this decision opened the door for Soviet influence in the region, which was the very situation that U.S. support for Israel was supposed to prevent. In retaliation for Nasser turning to the U.S.S.R., Eisenhower subsequently refused financial backing for Egypt's Aswan Dam project, again forcing Nasser to approach the Soviets for help and further cementing Soviet influence in the region. Although Egypt eventually realigned with the U.S. in the 1970s, America spent the next thirty-six years countering the Soviet influence in the region. During this period, Israel defeated Soviet-backed Arab states in three wars thus cementing the popular notion that Israel was indeed a "strategic asset" in the fight against Soviet expansion, regardless of the reason the Soviets gained influence there in the first place. Whatever the popular sentiment may have been regarding Israel as a strategic asset during this period, not everyone privately agreed. As Smith relates, "[President] Johnson encouraged [a settlement between Israel and the Arabs prior to the 1967 war] out of fear that the United States might be forced to intervene on behalf of Israel if war erupted; this in turn fed on apprehension that the Russians would intervene on behalf of the Arabs, inducing a great power conflict…"[127] This line of reasoning belies Johnson's realization that Israel was not, in fact, a strategic asset.

American support to Israel during the Cold War also added tension to the Arab-Israeli conflict and may have actually prolonged it. According to Mearsheimer and Walt, at least one opportunity was missed to bring an end to the conflict:

> …the tendency to view Middle East issues through the prism of the Cold War
>
> (and thus to back Israel no matter what) also led the United States to overlook
>
> several promising opportunities for peace, most notably Egyptian President

Anwar Sadat's repeated signals that he was prepared to cut a deal 1971-72.

Speaking to a group in 1975, Kissinger recalled that Secretary of State William

Roger's efforts to reach an interim agreement in 1971 had broken down 'over

whether or not 1,000 Egyptian soldiers would be permitted across the Canal. That

agreement would have prevented the 1973 war.'[128]

If U.S. foreign policy in the Middle East was aimed at promoting stability and peace,

unwavering support of Israel appears to have successfully prevented the realization of

that goal and may even be considered a contributing factor in driving Arab sentiment for

the U.S. further toward anti-Americanism.

Between World War I and 1948, America was not considered imperialist, as were

Britain and France according to Mearsheimer and Walt; however, subsequent U.S.

support of Middle Eastern monarchies created by Britain as well as deepening ties with

Israel in the 1960s and 1970s "fueled a growing tendency for many Arabs to see

[America] as the heir to Britain's former Imperial role."[129] As Mearsheimer and Walt

succinctly summarize: "Arab animosity increased as U.S. support for Israel grew and was

compounded by Israel's occupation of the West Bank, Sinai, Gaza, and the Golan

Heights in 1967 and by its subsequent repression of the Palestinian Arabs living in what

came to be known as the Occupied Territories."[130] This animosity persists today as

indicated in a March 21, 2013 interview conducted by Martin Fletcher, an NBC News

correspondent, with a Palestinian man in Ramallah, Israel. During the interview, Mustafa

al Khteeb says, "I cannot feed my children. I feel like half a man. This is a shame. I

blame President Obama."[131] Fletcher asked al Khteeb why he blamed America and not

his own country or Israel and al Khteeb replied "Because Israel does what America tells it to do and America is on the side of Israel."[132] It is this popular Arab sentiment that contributes to Islamic extremism according to Mearsheimer and Walt.[133]

Yet another product of U.S. support to Israel during the Cold War, the Arab oil embargo in the 1970s imposed on the U.S. a substantial cost above the benefit provided by Israel as a strategic asset. The embargo was a direct result of President Nixon's $2.2 billion military assistance package to Israel during the 1973 war. Mearsheimer and Walt note that the economic cost of the embargo to the U.S. was $48.5 billion in 1974 dollars and also included political costs as U.S. alliances in Europe suffered setbacks due to the American responsibility for the embargo, which affected the entire world.[134] The financial and political cost to America for supporting Israel in countering Soviet influence in Egypt and Syria in the 1970s was substantial, calling into question the validity of Israel as a strategic asset.

Classifying Israel as a strategic asset after the Cold War is similarly problematic. Even as early as the Gulf War in 1991, just prior to the collapse of the Soviet Union, Israel was anything but a strategic asset to the U.S. In the effort to free Kuwait from Iraqi occupation, the U.S. led a coalition of more than 400,000 international troops. Notably absent from the coalition was Israel, sequestered at the behest of the U.S. in order to maintain the alliance against Iraq, which included Arab states. America was equally unable to use Israeli territory as a staging area or base for troops, which effectively pushed the U.S. to forward deploy in Saudi Arabia. When Saddam Hussein attacked Israel with SCUD missiles during the war, the U.S. again forced Israel to remain out of the fray and not defend itself for fear of losing the backing of Arab coalition members. It was clear that even had Israel been a strategic asset prior to the end of the Cold War, this was no longer the case as of 1991. The Gulf War had gone a long way toward proving that Israel was at best irrelevant and at worst a strategic liability as the U.S. struggled to maintain the coalition.[135]

Another usual reason for describing Israel as a strategic asset post-Cold War is countering radical Islam and terror. As Mearsheimer and Walt point out, proponents of this rationale see Israel not as the source of American problems with the Arab world and Islam but as a "key ally" in the fight against terror.[136] This line of reasoning is similarly an axiom in American politics and is backed up by a robust Israeli effort to link the two nations together in the anti-terror effort. During a visit to the U.S. in 2001 after the attacks of September 11, Ariel Sharon remarked to American officials: "You in America are in a war against terror. We in Israel are in a war against terror. It's the same war."[137] Benjamin Netanyahu, the current Israeli Prime Minister, addressed the U.S. Senate in 2002: "If we do not immediately shut down the terror factories where [Yasser] Arafat is producing human bombs, it is only a matter of time before suicide bombers will terrorize your cities."[138] In 2002, resolutions passed both houses of the U.S. Congress declaring in part: "…the United States and Israel are now engaged in a common struggle against terrorism."[139] What these passages from leaders of both the U.S. and Israel make clear is that there exists the perception of a common strategic purpose; however, when the situations both states find themselves in are examined closely, Israel's strategic "ally" position with the U.S. falters and again more closely resembles the likeness of a strategic liability.

As the Zionists sought to expand the homeland they desired in Palestine in 1945-1948, Jewish forces regularly engaged in terrorism as they attempted to push the British and subsequently the Palestinians out of Palestine. Menachem Begin, future Prime Minister of Israel, led the Irgun in a terror attack on the King David Hotel in Jerusalem that killed ninety-one people in 1946.[140] In 1948, the LEHI, or Stern Gang, assassinated Folke Bernadotte, the U.N. mediator assigned to Arab-Israeli negotiations in the 1948 war.[141] In perhaps one of the most violent terrorist attacks the Jews ever committed, a joint Irgun-LEHI unit murdered and mutilated the bodies of around 250 men, women, and children in the Palestinian village of Dayr Yasin on April 9, 1948.[142] This attack was part of the Jewish campaign between April and May of 1948 to take over as much Palestinian land as possible before partition was declared by the U.N on May 15.[143] These examples are merely illustrative of the tactics used by Jews against adversaries at the time, whether British or Arab, but they provide context to the creation of Palestinian groups labeled as terrorist organizations by the U.S. and Israel in the 1960s and 1970s such as the PLO, Hezbollah, and Hamas. These Palestinian groups formed in direct response to Israel's occupation of Palestinian land and Israeli's use of terror to drive the Palestinian-Arabs from it.[144] In summary, the terrorist organizations that attack Israel do so because of very specific grievances against the Israeli government; chiefly, Israeli use of terror against Palestinians, Israeli occupation of Palestinian land, and continued Israeli settlement of Palestinian land in the West Bank and Jerusalem.[145] The terrorists that attack the U.S. are not only different from those that attack Israel but they attack for different reasons.

The terrorists who attack America do so because of overwhelming historical U.S. support for Israel. Mearsheimer and Walt suggest that American policies, which lopsidedly support Israel against her Arab neighbors, are to blame for al Qaeda's attacks against U.S. targets.[146] The authors make the following point:

> ...claiming that Israel and the United States are united by a shared terrorist threat has the causal relationship backward. The United States did not form an alliance with Israel because it suddenly realized that it faced a serious danger from 'global terrorism' and urgently needed Israel's help to defeat it. In fact, the United States has a terrorism problem in good part because it has long been so supportive of Israel.[147]

It was America's support of Israel, financially, politically, and militarily, which led al Qaeda to attack the U.S.[148]

Al Qaeda conducted four attacks against U.S. targets between 1993 and September 11, 2001. These attacks in order are the first World Trade Center (WTC) attack in 1993; the 1998 bombings of U.S. Embassies in Kenya and Tanzania; the 2000 attack on the USS Cole; and the attacks of September 11, 2001 on the WTC and the Pentagon. Ramzi Yousef, affiliated with al Qaeda through his uncle, 9/11 mastermind Khalid Sheikh Mohammed, carried out the first attack against the WTC in 1993 as part of a cell that also included Nidal Ayyad. Ayyad was a naturalized American citizen of Palestinian heritage from Kuwait. Educated at Rutgers University in New Jersey and possessing a degree in chemical engineering, Nidal acted as the cell's spokesman after the attack. In a letter to the New York Times after the attack, Ayyad stated: "This action was done in response for the American political, economical, and military support to Israel..."[149] Yousef, captured in Pakistan in 1995, talked with FBI agents and confirmed that U.S. foreign policies that supported Israel were his only motivation for the attack.[150] According to Coll, Yousef indicated he did not like killing Americans and felt guilty but that his conscience was "overridden by the strength of his desire to stop the killing of Arabs by Israeli troops."[151] Coll further indicates that Yousef believed his attack on the WTC was the only way to change U.S. policy toward Israel and thus stop Israel's killing of Arabs and Palestinians.[152]

Osama bin Laden, late leader of al Qaeda, was "deeply sympathetic" to the Palestinians and their cause and "angry at the United States for backing Israel so strongly," according to Mearsheimer and Walt.[153] Bin Laden outlined his personal and religious beliefs regarding the Palestinian issue in a statement to the public at large on December 29, 1994. The chronicler of bin Laden's public writings, Bruce Lawrence, indicates that "[This] letter makes it plain that Palestine, far from being a late addition to bin Laden's agenda, was at the centre of it from the start."[154] Bin Laden also referenced U.S. support to Israel in a 1996 'fatwa' titled *Declaration of War Against the Americans Occupying the Land of the Two Holy Places*. Benjamin and Simon indicate that the "most prominent grievance" given by bin Laden in the 'fatwa' is the American-Israeli alliance.[155] In perhaps the most direct connection between al Qaeda's terror attacks on the U.S. and American support of Israel, bin Laden himself outlines the causal relationship: During an interview with CNN's Peter Arnett in 1997, Arnett asked why bin Laden declared jihad against America. Bin Laden answered, "We declared jihad against the US government, because the US government is unjust, criminal, and tyrannical. It has committed acts that are extremely unjust, hideous, and criminal, whether directly or through its support of the Israeli occupation of the Land of the Prophet's Night Journey [Palestine]."[156]

Evidence suggests that those terrorist organizations that attack the U.S. justify their deeds as necessary in order to change American policy toward Israel. Although Hezbollah, Hamas, and other Palestinian organizations attack Israeli targets in order to change Israeli policies of occupation and settlement, the similarities between their agenda and al Qaeda's ends there. One attacks to change Israeli policy and the other attacks to change U.S. policy and, although the distinction between the two may appear small, it is quite important and factual. The U.S. and Israel are not fighting the same war on terror, as Ariel Sharon argued in 2001. Neither country is fighting a war on terror since the very label of a "war on terror" is entirely inaccurate; it is not possible to wage war on a line of effort. Wars are fought against people and Israel is fighting against the people whom it expelled from Palestine in 1948 and 1967 and continues to oppress. The U.S. is fighting groups determined to alter U.S. policy toward Israel and end American support to the Israeli cause. Thus, the strategic cost of maintaining an unconditional alliance with Israel is quite high when the al Qaeda attacks against America are tallied. If a causal line is drawn between U.S. support to Israel and the war in Afghanistan via the al Qaeda connection, then the cost of our "strategic partner" becomes truly remarkable. The alleged benefit of this alliance is touted as a "partner in the war on terror" yet it is that very partnership which has pulled the U.S. into a costly war. The only tangible benefit the U.S. appears to gain from the "strategic" partnership with Israel is limited assistance fighting terrorists that the partnership helped create.

Conclusion

The Arab world watches as the U.S. steadfastly supports Israel and provides tacit approval while Israel refuses to recognize the boundaries set by the U.N. in 1947 and offers little indication of withdrawing from the West Bank. Arabs see hypocrisy in the historic U.S. support of Israel, a state that used terrorism to eject Palestinians from their homeland and continues to oppress the remaining Palestinian population using American weapons, technology, and financing.[157] U.S. foreign policy decisions with regard to Israel and the Palestinians are seen as unbalanced and heavily in favor of Israel. As Mearsheimer and Walt note, "These [U.S.] policies help explain why many Arabs and Muslims are so angry with the United States that they regard al Qaeda with sympathy."[158] Shibley Telhami, a Middle Eastern authority, agrees: "No other issue resonates with the public in the Arab world, and many other parts of the Muslim world, more deeply than Palestine. No other issue shapes the regional perceptions of America more fundamentally than the issue of Palestine."[159] These Arab perceptions of the U.S. help energize groups like al Qaeda and have led to growing anti-U.S. sentiment in the Arab world and evidence strongly suggests that American support for Israel is the root cause. What strategic value, if any, the U.S. receives from continuous, unmitigated support to Israel is far outweighed by the actual financial cost as well as the unrelenting anti-Americanism prevalent throughout the Middle East. Labeling Israel a strategic asset to the U.S. is questionable when considering that what little strategic value exists comes from limited Israeli help combating the very terror organizations the alliance helped create. It is a circular argument. Perhaps King Ibn Saud of Saudi Arabia best summed up the cost of a U.S.-Israeli alliance when he remarked to President Truman in 1947 "[U.S. support for partition in Palestine would be a] deathblow to American interests in the Arab countries."[160] After giving Israel over $115 billion[161] since 1948, provoking Soviet influence in the Middle East which almost brought the U.S. to the brink of nuclear war in 1973, suffering multiple attacks by al Qaeda, and fighting a costly war in Afghanistan to counter radical Islam, the reality lies closer to the characterization of Israel as a strategic liability. Perhaps a more even-handed approach to U.S. foreign policy in the Middle East, a policy that recognizes the significant strategic benefits of support to and cooperation with the Arab states, would provide a much more real strategic benefit and reduce the economic and military cost to the Unites States in the future.